Letters to Will Series

Letter 4: What Is Buddhism?

By Leonard Swidler, PhD

About iPubCloud.com

iPubCloud.com is the Digital Publishing arm of iPub Global Connection, LLC. Focusing on globally transformative books from authors all over the world, we value and help promote the works of creators who influence our world in matters of equality, interfaith dialogue, psychology, philosophy, and planet sustainability.

Our value to you is simplicity and convenience. The continually curated book list is culled from the New York Times, Amazon reader reviews and iPub subject matter advisors. You may be confident when you select an item from our store; everything is fulfilled by Amazon, its affiliates, and other important distribution channels.

There are many books like this one on iPubCloud.com along with selections of other categories of books. Don't keep us a secret. Connect with us on Facebook and join our mailing list. And, if you have a story to tell, reach out.

iPub Global Connection, LLC
www.iPubCloud.com
550 W. Baseline Rd., #303
Mesa, AZ 85210
info@iPubCloud.com
Copyright © 2019 Leonard Swidler
ISBN 978-1-948575-12-6

Cover Design by Arewa Abiodun Ibrahim
Cover Image by Sudowoodo Shutterstock.com

Contents

Introduction

"Will" is short for Willow Athena Swidler-Notte, my fantastic granddaughter, born at the beginning of the Third Millennium (2000), to whose house I have been going practically every weekend since 2011, to teach her German (which is why I am addressed as *Opa*, a typical German abbreviation for Grandpa), and slowly talk about all kinds of exciting things in life – and end up having a vegetarian dinner with Will and my brilliant daughter Eva and her wonderful husband Ian (both are professors, Ian high school ecology/biology, and Eva university history).

These are my letters to Will, with whom – when you meet her, you will understand why – I clearly am madly in love.

Opa, Len   Len Swidler (<ins>info@ipubcloud.com</ins>)

Letter No. 4: What Is Buddhism?

Dear Will,

There are two explanations that you should know about before we begin. For one, you will see little numbers that look like they are connected to a word. These are called footnotes. If you click on the number, a window will open and give you additional information where you can find even more information about what you just read. (Or, look to the bottom of the printed page.) Fun, isn't it?

Another important explanation is how we came to refer to Bible verses and to show them in books that I write. A little bit of background before I describe the method. The word Bible was derived from the ancient Phoenician (present-day Lebanon) coastal city, Byblos, where the papyrus reeds from along the Nile river in Egypt were shipped to be pressed and transformed into "paper" (papyrus), sheets of which, when sewn together formed a "book" (from Byblos).

The Bible for Jews consists of the Torah. [Hebrew word for "teaching"]

The Bible for Christians consists of the "Old Testament"—today, out of respect for the Jewish tradition and the "New Testament consisting of the four Gospels:

- Matthew
- Mark
- Luke
- John

The four Gospels:

- Writings about the Jew Yeshua [Hebrew for Jesus]
- Paul of Tarsus' letters
- Other early missionaries' writings referring to Jesus as the "Messiah" [In Hebrew: Meshiach and in Greek: Christos meaning the Anointed One.]

References to both the Hebrew Bible and the New Testament are usually presented by an abbreviated form of the subsection, called a "book," followed by the chapter number, and then the verses.

For example, the first book of the Bible, Genesis, would be cited this way:

"Gen 3: 5-9"

The biblical book, Genesis, chapter 3, verses 5 to 9.

I hope this explanation helps you reading this book and the Bible easier. And, as we always say, Will, *Wir werden sehen*! [German for we will see!]

You wrote and asked me to explain to you what Buddhism is all about because, from what you heard about it, you find it confusing and at times strange. Well, Will, I know exactly what you mean, because that was largely my own experience when

I first learned about Buddhism many, many decades ago.

Buddha taught that all life was suffering, that the cause of suffering was desire, and that we can get rid of suffering by getting rid of its cause, desire. Well, that didn't make any sense, as I will explain a bit more below. However, let me first start with the very name: Buddhism.

1. **Siddhartha Gautama, the Buddha**

The name "Buddha" is a Sanskrit word meaning *"enlightened one,"* and is a title given to Siddhartha Gautama, a prince in northern India who lived around 500 BCE. His father "spoiled" him terribly, arranging for Siddhartha (I call him Sid for short) to marry a beautiful woman, with whom he had a child. He seemed to be on his way to becoming the eventual successor to his father and "live happily ever after"—as in the zillion fairy tales I read to you, Will! However, the story is told that one day he saw a funeral pass by with a terrible looking corpse, which led him to investigate and learn that everybody eventually got sick and died— Oh my god! What a shock!

Well, Will, you remember that in my first letter we talked all about the "meaning of life." That became a burning question for Sid, and he asked around to find out how he could learn the "meaning of life." He decided to leave his palace and family to join a group of wandering ascetics—guys who pretty much lived in the wild and ate as little as they possibly could without actually dying. Here is one artist's image of what he must have looked like:

Pretty gruesome looking, huh!?

Well, before we move on to serious issues, let me show you one more photo, which is very interesting. But first a little background. Will, have you heard of the

Christian teaching of the "Virgin Birth"? Very often people, and even learned scholars, get it mixed up with the Christian teaching of the: "*Virginal Conception*," that is, that Jesus was conceived in Mary's womb without sexual intercourse, by the will of the Holy Spirit. The teaching of the "*Immaculate* Conception," on the other hand, is that *Mary* was conceived without "stain" [*macula* in Latin, hence, *im*maculate] of Original Sin. The teaching of the Virgin *Birth* is that Jesus was *born* of Mary without destroying her virginity—that is, without her hymen being broken (which is the traditional "proof" that a woman had not had sexual intercourse.)

Now, Will, you might think that being so concerned about a woman's hymen— especially since there are many ways that it can be broken other than sexual intercourse—as from horseback riding,

11

for example—is a bit weird, especially when the ones doing the worrying were celibate males. But there are a number of weird things in the world, and a lot of them have to do with sex. So, in fact, in the tenth century some Christian theologians—male, of course—started to worry about Jesus being born without breaking Mary's hymen, and came up with the teaching that Jesus must have had a "Virginal Birth"; that is, he was born without breaking Mary's hymen.

The presumption was put forward that Jesus passed through Mary's hymen without breaking it, like light passes through glass without breaking it. Neat, eh, Will? But, when asked how they knew that it actually happened that way, they said, in Latin: *Decet, ergo fecit*, "It is decent, becoming, therefore it happened." I know, Will, you are thinking, they had no proof; they simply assumed because they thought it was becoming, it happened. Not at all persuasive, you would say, Will.

But guess what, Christian theologians were not the only ones who thought this way about "Virgin Birth," birth with unbroken hymens. So, too, did certain Buddhists about Siddhartha and his mother. Here is a picture of how they imagined it happened:[1]

---

[1]https://images.search.yahoo.com/search/images?p=photo+of+b irth+of+Buddha&fr=tightropetb&imgurl=https%3A%2F%2Fu pload.wikimedia.org%2Fwikipedia%2Fcommons%2Ff%2Fff% 2FBirth_of_buddha_peshawar.JPG#id=23&iurl=http%3A%2F %2Fwww.hinduwebsite.com%2Fbuddhism%2Fimages%2Fbud dha-birth.jpg&action=click.

See, little Sid is coming out the *side* of his

mother, not breaking her hymen. Now, of course, Buddhists do not claim that Siddhartha was conceived virginally, as some Christians did later for Jesus, but that he was *born* virginally. Obviously, this was something that distinguished Siddhartha from all the rest of us, made him special—which, of course, was the same idea with Jesus: *decet ergo fecit*!

2. Buddha's Four Noble Truths

Back to serious matters, Will. After a number of years of trying to learn the "meaning of life" by avoiding all bodily pleasures (you remember our earlier discussion of "extreme dualism" which teaches that matter is bad and only spirit is good), Sid decided—after almost dying from starvation—that this route led nowhere. So, as the story goes, he sat down under what eventually was called a *Bodhe* [Sanskrit for "Enlightenment"] Tree and meditated hours and days on end... until, one day, he "got it"! He became "enlightened"! He then spelled out his enlightened insight in what has become known as the "Four Noble Truths"—the gist of which I gave at the beginning of this letter:

1) All life is suffering [Sanskrit, *dukkha*].

2) The cause of suffering is desire.

3) Get rid of suffering by getting rid of desire.

4) To do so, follow the eightfold path.

Well, Will, I don't have to explain to you that all that seemed like nonsense to me then. First of all, I did not think that all life is suffering. If eating at ice cream sundaes at Dehn's Restaurant (a fantastic ice cream parlor hangout of mine in Green Bay in the late 1930s and early 1940s) was "suffering," then I thought, "Bring it on!"

Further, the solution to getting rid of *dukkha* by eliminating its cause, "desire," seemed even more wrong-headed to me. If we eliminated all desire, as I wrote you earlier, Will, we would all very quickly be dead. If we did not follow our desire for food, for example, we would all die of starvation (as Sid nearly did!). It seemed like the cure for a headache being offered was beheading! Not a very attractive explanation of the meaning of life!

That unattractive, weird explanation of Buddhism all evaporated for me, however, a number of years ago, when I received in the mail a copy of a book by a Catholic priest, Antony Fernando, who had a doctorate in Catholic theology from Rome and a doctorate in Buddhist studies from the Sorbonne in Paris.[2] The letter came from Sri Lanka, where most people are Buddhist.

First of all, Antony made it clear that the *dukkha* Sid was talking about was recognizing that not only would bad things stop, so would good things. For example, somewhere during a "happy" (*sukkha* in Sanskrit) vacation the thought will intrude that it is going to end, that

---

[2] The book title is *Buddhism Made Plain for Christians*. I eventually helped rewrite it and get it published under the title *Buddhism Made Plain for Christians and Jews* (iPub Global Connection, LLC 2018).

sooner or later the work week will start again. That is *dukkha*, and the "great" *dukkha* is that our whole life will also come to an end at the grave.

I learned also that Sid was twenty-five hundred years ahead of our twentieth century molecular science in arguing that *everything* in the world is changing, fleeting. For example, Will, I am sure you learned from your Dad's biology instructions that there won't be a single molecule in your body seven years from now that is there today! Sid had a Sanskrit word for fleeting: *anicca*. This is an important part of the solution to understanding Sid's "Four Noble Truths."

A third key is that the Sanskrit for the word that traditionally has been translated into English as "desire" is *tanha*, which really means, not "desire," but "clinging," "grasping." Aha! Now it should begin to fall in place: Reality is not static, it is totally "fleeting," *anicca*; when we make the mistake of trying to *tanha* (grasp) the present reality, which is *anicca*, (fleeting) we get—guess what, Will?—*dukkha*, (suffering)! A good analogy would be as if you were standing next to a running creek and put your hand in to try to hold the water back, stop it from being *anicca*—the result would be that the water would just run through your fingers—frustration, suffering, *dukkha*!

Ah, Will, now you can see what Sid was trying to say: If you try to *tanha* (grasp) reality, which is *anicca*, you will inevitably get *dukkha* for your efforts. Therefore, if you want to avoid *dukkha...* Silence.... OK, Will, you might be thinking, "Opa, that sounds pretty much like how our cat Cynthia lives, from moment to moment— but surely we humans are looking for much more than what our cat seems to understand!" Right, and there is a lot more to Buddhism.

3. Karma, the Moral Law of Cause and Effect: Hinduism and Buddhism

For starters, most traditional Buddhists, like Sid, assume the Indian idea of *karma*, which I explain to my university students as the "moral version of the physical law of cause and effect": Every cause has a strictly proportionate effect.

I use the example, Will, if you and I were in a row boat on a lake and we decided to go for a swim. When you dove off the side of the boat, it would rock back a certain amount according to your weight; when I dove off, the boat would rock back even more, in proportion to how much more I weigh than you. Well, *karma* is like that, according to Indian religions; that is, you do X amount of morally good things in your life, and Y amount of morally bad things, and you are "rewarded" in just proportion—like the boat rocking back proportionately. But you are no doubt thinking that lots of people do many

21

good things, but are poor, whereas lots of other people do many bad things, but are rich! Not fair! Where is the *karma*? Well, Indian religion has an answer for that as well. But that will take another paragraph to explain, so come with me a little further.

Will, you have read a lot about ancient peoples, how they all looked for the meaning of life, and that they came up with varying understandings, as well as explanations of where everything came from—in brief, answers to two questions: Whence and Whither?[3] Well, as you know, the people living in what we today call India got that name from the Indus river in what today is Pakistan. They were one of the four ancient civilizations: 1. Fertile Crescent of Mesopotamia and Egypt, 2. Indus Valley, 3. Yellow River Valley in China, and 4. Greece.

---

[3] Barbara C. Sproul, *Primal Myths. Creation Myths around the World* (New York: Harper, 1979) describes and analyzes hundreds of creation and related myths from around the world.

This is going to sound a little complicated because it is so different from what we grow up with in the West, but just stick with it a little, and you will begin to see that it is not really all that different.

The ancient Indians came up with the idea that there is one Ultimate Reality, the source of everything that exists, which they called *Brahman*, which is pretty much what Judaism, Christianity, and Islam (often referred to as "Abrahamic Religions" because all three look to Abraham as their spiritual "Father") call God, the Source of everything. The Indians thought of *Brahman* both as simply "Being Itself," which they called *Brahman Nirguna* [*nirguna* in Sanskrit means "*no* attributes," like "just," "knowing," "merciful," "powerful"]. However, Will, somewhat different, but not completely, from the Abrahamic religions, the Indians also thought that *Brahman* manifested itself in the world in various forms, like being "just" and "kind," and at times took specific forms, such as *Vishnu* and *Krishna*. These are not different "gods," but various "manifestations," [*avatar* in Sanskrit]. The Indians said that all these "gods" were really the one and only *Brahman*, and then in these cases they name it *Brahman Saguna* [Sanskrit for "some attributes"].

Just as the Abrahamic religions taught that God is the source of everything, so the Indians in effect said the same thing, and instead of using the name *God*, or *Gott*, or *Dieu*, or *Deos*.... They used the term *Brahman*. They taught that since we all came from *Brahman*, the goal of life is for our spirit [*atman* in Sanskrit, which interestingly means "breath," just as *spiritus* in Latin means "breath"—that is, no *spiritus/atman*, no life!] ultimately to return to its Source, God/*Brahman*.

Now, Will, here is where *karma* comes in. What about the person who has a pretty easy life, but badly misuses it? It would not be just of *Brahman* to reward that person with a joyful union with *Brahman*. However, Will, the Indians were convinced that if something existed, it never went out of existence. So, for example, when a tree's life is destroyed by lightning, it does not just disappear. Rather, it decomposes into its various parts and other plants grow from it. Well, Indians and a lot of other people think that this is not so terribly bad. Things in life need to balance out.

You know, Will, simple Christians and Muslims talk about just persons going to heaven or paradise to be with God when they die; but if they were really bad, they go to hell, or if they were "in between" they go to purgatory. That's how traditional Abrahamic religions handled the problem of ultimate justice in the world.

I know, I know, you are itching to know where the *karma* comes in that I promised to tell you about! Well, the Indians didn't figure that justice would be balanced out in some kind of different existence after the grave— like the Christian solutions of Heaven, Purgatory, Hell—they figured it would all have to be taken care of on this earth, after the grave. Will, this is the very different solution that the Indians came up with: "Reincarnation." They figured that your spirit, *atman*, would exit its body at death and then go into a new body. Remember, Will, *carne* in its root Latin means "flesh," so "re-in-carnate" literally means "again in flesh." Moreover, the Indians said that you will be reincarnated precisely according to your good and bad *karma* in the life you have just finished—all of which seems pretty fair so far.

Will, you are probably a bit set back on your heels just now with this literally quite "outlandish" notion, but I know you, and am sure that soon your next question is going to be: How often can/must a spirit/*atman* go through another life, starting out all over again as an infant, living.... dying—oh wow!? Now we are really coming close to the "purpose of life" according to Indian thought. They speak of this cycle of birth-life-death-rebirth-life....as *samsara*, which in Sanskrit means "cycle." The point of life, the Indians said, is to break this *samsara*, this cycle of birth-life-death-rebirth..... The breaking of *samsara* they call *moksha*, which in Sanskrit means "release," from the "samsaric" cycle so that one can return to the source of one's existence, *Brahman*— which return is called *nirvana*.

So, to try to sum up what we learned so far about traditional Indian thought, some parts are quite like the Abrahamic religions' thought, except for the reincarnation solution to the requirement of justice: There is one God (*Brahman*, who is manifested in various *avatar*s) who creates everything that exists. Each being has an *atman* which is responsible for its morally good and bad actions (*karma*), and must be purified by way of one or many incarnations (the cycle of *samsara*) so as to be released (*moksha*) from the samsaric cycle so its *atman* can be reunited with *Brahman* (*nirvana*). Simple, eh, Will—after each term and their relationships have been clearly understood!

As you have noticed, Will, the last page or two was really about Buddhism's parent, Hinduism. What Siddhartha accepted from Hinduism are the notions of *karma, samsara, moksha*, and *nirvana*. However, Sid did not accept the idea of an originating/final goal *Brahman*—but he also did not directly say that there is no Ultimate, no *Brahman*, or God in the Abrahamic sense. He simply refused to ask the question.

Well, I know you are thinking: Wait a moment! What is *nirvana* for Siddhartha if he doesn't start and end with *Brahman*? Well, of course, he doesn't say, because most of what he teaches is "negative," that is, largely: Don't grasp, *tanha*, don't do harmful things, as in, for example, the widely-held Indian (including Buddhist) teaching of *ahimsa*, "no harm."

Sid wasn't like a standard Western atheist, however, who says that when humans die they simply ceases to exist—which is called *nihilism*, "nothing-ness." No, Sid simply says that the human who achieves *nirvana* will exist "blissfully." Hmm, what do you think, Will, sounds quite a bit like a more "level-headed" Christian description of heaven, doesn't it?

Well, as we all know, we just don't *know* what comes after the grave: heaven, hell, reincarnation, *nirvana*, nothing.... We each have our "beliefs," our hopes, which has given rise to our different "religions" or other explanations. However, we don't *know*. As a well-known Chicago Bears football player with a terminal disease said when asked whether he was afraid of dying: "Well, yes, I never died before." (He clearly was not a believing Hindu or Buddhist!)

Will, what I have laid out here is the "essence" of Siddhartha's teaching, which we call Buddhism. Of course, a lot happened to his core teaching over the millennia since his death. However, we'll save all that for another letter!

I hope that I have answered some of your basic questions about Buddhism, and that it doesn't seem so weird—as it at first did to me—but now seems to make a lot of, though not complete, sense...along with all the other "explanations of the total meaning of life, whether one of the so-called "religions," or some other "explanation."

Dein,

Opa

Do Not Miss Out

Other Books in the Series

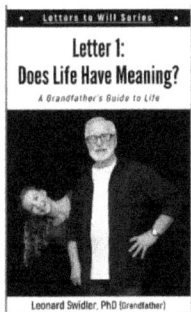

Letters to Will Series
Letter 1:
Does Life Have Meaning?
A Grandfather's Guide to Life
Leonard Swidler, PhD (Grandfather)

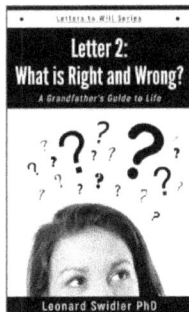

Letters to Will Series
Letter 2:
What is Right and Wrong?
A Grandfather's Guide to Life
Leonard Swidler PhD

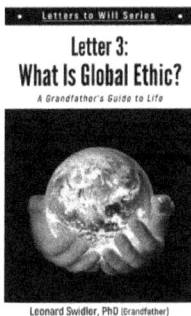

Letters to Will Series
Letter 3:
What Is Global Ethic?
A Grandfather's Guide to Life
Leonard Swidler, PhD (Grandfather)

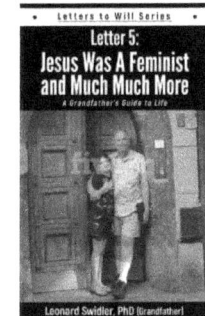

Letters to Will Series
Letter 5:
Jesus Was A Feminist and Much Much More
A Grandfather's Guide to Life
Leonard Swidler, PhD (Grandfather)